# Praise for *Take It to Heart*

Rachel Schmoyer's love for Scripture shines through in this devoted offering. The author of Hebrews assures us God's word is living and powerful, partnering with us in redemptive work now, not only looking toward eternity. Rachel embraces this truth, studying Revelation not as glimpses into a future time, but as a book with lessons, and opportunities for worship, today. *Take It to Heart* is a wonderful mix of teaching, personal narrative, and opportunities for reflection.

—**Traci Rhoades**, author of *Not All Who Wander (Spiritually) Are Lost*

Rachel is known for her passion to lead women to the Word. Here she shows how Revelation, far from being scary, is meant to be a comfort and a challenge to God's people. Rachel has a fine grasp on the Bible text and presents it in warm, sympathetic, and moving ways, drawn from her own life.

—**Gary S. Shogren**, PhD in New Testament Exegesis, University of Aberdeen

Rachel Schmoyer's *Take It to Heart: 30 Days through Revelation* provides a sigh of relief to those wanting to apply the Bible's Book of Revelation to ordinary daily life.

—**Michelle Ule,** 35-year Bible study leader; speaker and author of *Mrs. Oswald Chambers: The Woman behind the World's Bestselling Devotional.* www.michelleule.com

Rachel Schmoyer has already proven she doesn't shy away from the hard parts of Scripture, but she also proves in *Take It to Heart: 30 Days through Revelation* that she can gently walk readers into the hardest parts of Scripture. Writing and speaking in the "prophecy world" for the past several years has shown me that teachers want to immediately drag their students into the deep water of end-time prophecy, but in *Take It to Heart,* Schmoyer is content not to overwhelm the reader while being true to the text and not shying away from challenging them. This devotional is a great tool for those new to the study of Revelation and for those who have spent a lifetime in the book.

—**Jake McCandless**, executive director of Stand Firm Ministries & Prophecy Simplified; lead pastor of Epic Church

I'm so delighted to endorse this title on Revelation. Rachel has taken on various hard parts of Scripture over the last few years and broken them down into applicable, practical devotions that train and edify others. *Take It to Heart: 30 Days through Revelation* continues to build on the work she has been doing and is a title I will be recommending to my friends and family!

—**Victoria Duerstock**, award winning author of the Heart & Home books with Abingdon Press and new releases *Extraordinary Hospitality for Ordinary Christians* and *Advent Devotions & Christmas Crafts for Families* with Skyhorse Publishing

# Take It to Heart

30 DAYS THROUGH REVELATION,
A DEVOTIONAL WORKBOOK FOR WOMEN

## Rachel Schmoyer

CrossLink Publishing
RAPID CITY, SD

Schmoyer/CrossLink Publishing
1601 Mt. Rushmore Rd., Ste 3288
Rapid City, SD 57701
www.CrossLinkPublishing.com

Ordering Information:
Quantity sales. Special discounts are available on quantity purchases by corporations, associations, and others. For details, contact the "Special Sales Department" at the address above.

Take It to Heart / Rachel Schmoyer. —1st ed.
ISBN 978-1-63357-346-8
Library of Congress Control Number: 2020942995

*To Tim, for patiently listening to everything I take to heart. Thank you!*

*and*

*To Deb Davies, my cheerleader.*

# Contents

# Introduction

I never thought I would like spending time in the ocean. The water is cold and the waves are strong. I'd much rather sit in my comfortable chair in the warm sun. But during a recent beach vacation, my husband persuaded me to give the water a try. First, I let the water lap around my feet. Once I acclimated to the temperature, I took a step and let the water go up to my shins. It was cold! But gradually, one step at a time, I ventured further and further out into the ocean until I was bobbing in the waves with my husband and kids and actually enjoying it. The fun couldn't have happened without the first step.

This devotional book is my invitation for you to dip your toe into Revelation. This is not an exhaustive Bible study or an in-depth training on end-times events. This devotional will help you make sense of a Bible book punctuated with dragons and beasts and judgment. This book will show you what you can take to heart for your life today.

By reading Revelation, just like the rest of Scripture, we can know who God is and know how to live as believers in the world He created. Let's find out together what Jesus has revealed to us in the book of Revelation.

**How to Use This Book**

Each day for the next thirty days, read the portion of Revelation chosen for the day's Scripture reading. Next, read the key verse as well as the insights and information in the devotion. The "Take It to Heart" prayer sums up how the passage impacts your life today. The "Take It Further" section helps you connect Revelation to the broader context of Scripture and the Christian life.

This book can also be used for small groups. You can read five days' worth of devotions per week for a six-week study. Use the "Take It Further" questions as well as the additional discussion questions provided. You can also watch the optional short teaching videos at ReadtheHardParts.com/Revelation.

If you have questions or comments along the way, I'd love to hear from you. You can reach me through my website, ReadtheHardParts.com, or by connecting with me on Facebook, Twitter, or Instagram.

## Doctrinal Disclaimer

The focus of this book is not the timeline of end-time events. No matter what your view is on the tribulation or the millennial kingdom (or whether or not you've even heard those terms before) you will benefit from this book because the focus is on finding simple truth for today. If you are curious about my personal doctrinal beliefs, you can refer to the Articles of Faith of the Bible Fellowship Church, the evangelical denomination my local church is a part of, at BFC.org.

# Take It to Heart

**Scripture Reading**: Revelation 1:1–8

**Key Verse**
"Blessed is the one who reads aloud the words of this prophecy, and blessed are those who hear it and take to heart what is written in it, because the time is near." Revelation 1:3

**Devotion**
"Jesus is coming back. That's all I need to know."

Often this is the reason given when I ask someone why they don't want to read Revelation. Although the book does end with a glorious description of the victorious return of Christ, knowing the future is not the only reason to read Revelation.

God has given us Revelation as a gift for today. He is eagerly waiting for us to untie the bow on the box of Revelation by reading it, hearing it, and taking it to heart. In Greek, the original language used to write Revelation, the word for "to hear" means "to heed," or "pay attention to." We are to pay attention to what is written in Revelation— not just the end where Jesus returns, but the whole book. The word translated "take to heart" means "to keep," as in to obey a commandment. Although Revelation tells us what happens in the future, it also speaks into our Christian life today. God designed Revelation to impact our ordinary, everyday life.

2 Timothy 3:16–17 says, "All Scripture is God-breathed and is useful for teaching, rebuking, correcting and training in righteousness, so that the servant of God may be thoroughly equipped for every good work." Revelation is included in "all Scripture." Without reading Revelation we will not be thoroughly equipped for every good work. We will be missing tools from our toolbox for everyday life, like comfort, love, and rest in God's justice. We will miss out on descriptions of pure, heavenly worship to guide our worship on earth. We will lack urgency for sharing the gospel with our unbelieving family and friends.

God invites us to read and heed Revelation. Open its pages and feel God's love, comfort, and justice flood your heart. Let Revelation soak into your soul so you can be changed for today. This is the blessing of Revelation.

## Take It to Heart
Dear Lord, thank you for Revelation. May I take to heart what is written in it so that I may heed, obey, and be blessed by you. In Jesus's name, amen.

## Take It Further
Before you continue to read Revelation, write down what you already know about the book. Who is the author? What does it tell us about the future? What does it offer us for life today? What does it show us about God? Then, write down any questions you have about the book.

John is the author — sent to the island of Patmos + God gives him a vision — What will lead up to Christ's return then his 1000 yr. reign the great judgment seat — crowns or rewards given + Satan finally being cast into hell.

# Drawn to the Light

**Scripture Reading**: Revelation 1:9–20

**Key Verse**
"The hair on his head was white like wool, as white as snow, and his eyes were like blazing fire. His feet were like bronze glowing in a furnace, and his voice was like the sound of rushing waters." Revelation 1:14–15

**Devotion**
When I decorate for Christmas, I carefully place a wreath on the door, hang stockings on the fireplace mantel, weave garland around the banister, and spread out the Christmas tablecloth. I enjoy each of these decorations, but the Christmas tree gets the most attention. The bright white lights make the tree stand out in the midst of the other

red and green décor. All season long, as much as I can, I sit by the tree and bask in the glow while I read, eat cookies, or chat with my family.

When the apostle John was a young man, he heard Jesus call Himself the "light of the world" (John 8:12). When John writes Revelation, he is an old man, banished to the island of Patmos. It has been about sixty years since he saw Jesus, his Savior and friend, ascend into heaven. One day he hears, "Write this down." John whirls around to see who is speaking to him and sees Jesus, who is now literally light: white woolen hair, eyes like fire, glowing bronze feet, face like the shining sun! No wonder John fell at His feet in worship. Everything else faded from view as his attention was drawn to the brilliance of Jesus, the Light.

One day we, too, will literally see Jesus as the Light. In the new heaven and new earth there will be no sun; Jesus will provide the light (Rev. 21:23). Until then, we focus on Jesus, the Light of the World. Sometimes it is hard to keep this focus since we have other things clamoring for our attention. Stay focused on Jesus, who is the center of all things in this life and in eternity.

**Take It to Heart**
Dear Jesus, thank you for providing yourself as the Light. May we turn to you for warmth and guidance. In your name, amen.

**Take It Further**
In the space provided below, keep track of the descriptions of Jesus in the book of Revelation, starting with Jesus as the Light. Write down each description and find out where else in Scripture Jesus is described in a similar way. For example, write down Jesus as Light in Revelation 1:14–15. Then write John 8:12. You may want to draw each picture of Jesus instead. We will add to this page as we continue to read Revelation.

His face was like the Sun shining

Head & Hair, White like wool.
eyes like fire.
golden sash

out of his mouth a sharp double edged sword

7 golden lampstands

glowing bronze

# Your First Love: The Church of Ephesus

**Scripture Reading**: Revelation 2:1–7

**Key Verse**
"Yet I have this against you: you have forsaken the love you had at first." Revelation 2:4

**Devotion**
I remember the day I laid eyes on my first love. I was a young teen at summer camp. All of us girls were giggly about the boys. But there was one particular timid teen with big glasses and a serene smile who captured my attention.

Two years later, I was on staff at the summer camp and the timid boy was still there. Only now he had ditched the glasses, gotten a new haircut, and had an air of self-confidence that wasn't there before. Apparently, my bright red hair and silly sailor hat had captured his attention too. We began dating several weeks later while serving the Lord at the camp.

Five years later we were married. Eighteen years later, we are still married and still love each other, although I don't walk around with my heart aflutter all the time. My husband and I fill our schedules with everyday life. We drift into ho-hum seasons where we treat each other like ships passing in the night instead of lovers. Then something will remind me of the love we had at first. Warm feelings resurface on Valentine's Day, an anniversary, or while looking at old photos. *That's right*, I think, *I love this man!* The memories give me new motivation to live each day as a spouse in intentional love.

The church in Ephesus was going through the motions of faith. Same old, same old. Worshiping, doing good deeds, doing all the right things, but without the right heart behind it. They had forgotten the love they had at first. It had been a long time since they first fell in love with their Savior Jesus. Now, Jesus calls them to repent; to turn back to the day of their salvation and remember the love of Jesus. Looking back on their salvation day and remembering Jesus as their first love would infuse their Christian walk with new energy and vigor and love, as opposed to stoically going through the motions.

## Take It to Heart

Dear God, remind me of your love, which drew me to you. I want to serve you out of love and not out of habit. In Jesus's name, amen.

## Take It Further

Reminisce through your personal experiences with Jesus's love. Plot a line graph or create a timeline of the major events in your life that have caused you to fall more deeply in love with Him. When were you saved? What other times in your life have you deeply felt the love of God?

# The Reality of Riches: The Church of Smyrna

**Scripture Reading**: Revelation 2:8–11

**Key Verse**
"I know your afflictions and your poverty—yet you are rich!" Revelation 2:9a

**Devotion**
How much money does one need to have before declaring oneself rich? In an interview with wealthy people in Silicon Valley, a man with more than $2 million in the bank and a house worth

$1.3 million that overlooks the Pacific Ocean said, "A few million doesn't go as far as it used to."[1]

What?! If you're like me, you are probably thinking he's crazy. He has more money than ninety-eight percent of Americans, yet he does not feel rich. He is comparing himself to others who have more.

The believers who were part of the church of Smyrna did not feel rich either, but for good reason. They were in poverty here on earth. Their oppressors did not allow them to buy or sell because they were Christians. As a result, they had no way to earn a living or even get food. But Jesus did not promise to give them an abundant income. He also didn't promise to lift their oppression. Instead, he encouraged them to be faithful to the point of death. Despite their bleak prospects, Jesus declared them rich.

To be rich means to have abundance. In Christ, both the church of Smyrna and believers today are rich. We have been blessed "with every spiritual blessing in Christ" (Eph. 1:3). Nothing is held back. Being rich is a fact. Living in light of the riches you have in Christ gives confidence, assuages anxiousness, and gives rewards in heaven.

---

1  Gary Rivlin, "In Silicon Valley, Millionaires Who Don't Feel Rich," *New York Times*, 2007, https://www.nytimes.com/2007/08/05/technology/05rich.html, accessed July 1 2020.

In God's kingdom there is no monetary definition of what makes someone rich. Your checkbook on earth has no bearing on your heavenly riches. Being rich isn't relative. It's a reality.

**Take It to Heart**
Dear Father in heaven, thank you for the riches you have given to me in Christ. May I live in the reality of the riches you have given. In Jesus's name, amen.

**Take It Further**
Read Ephesians 1:3–14. Below, list the spiritual riches from the passage. What other verses in Scripture describe spiritual riches in Christ?

He chose us before the foundation of the world to be holy + blameless

He predestined us to be adopted as his sons in Jesus Christ

We have redemption through his blood

The forgiveness of sins

God's grace

He made known to us the mystery of His Will

We were marked in him a a seal, the promised Holy Spirit - guaranteeing our inheritance

# A New Name: The Church of Pergamum

**Scripture Reading**: Revelation 2:12–17

**Key Verse**
"To him who overcomes, to him I will give some of the hidden manna and I will give him a white stone, and a new name written on the stone which no one knows but he who receives it." Revelation 2:17b

**Devotion**
I am called by a variety of names. Mrs. Schmoyer at school. Miss Rachel to the kids at church. Mom to my kids. Rachel to my family and friends.

In this passage, there are a lot of names:

- **Satan** has been against God's plan since the beginning of time.

- **Antipas** was martyred, probably by a paganistic cult devoted to worshiping the emperor.

- **Balaam** was asked to curse the Israelites. While God wouldn't allow the curse, Balaam suggested **Balak** destroy the Israelites by tempting them with sexual immorality and food sacrificed to idols (Num. 22–24; 31).

- The **Nicolatians** were false teachers who were swaying some of the church of Pergamum away from the truth.

In the midst of these proper names, two people are referred to indirectly. Jesus is called the one with the sharp, two-edged sword. Individual believers are "the one who overcomes." God will reward each overcomer with a white stone inscribed with their new name.

I imagine myself at the gates of heaven, holding out my hand while Jesus places a cool white stone in my palm. I touch the smooth surface and flip over the stone to peek at my new name, a secret name known only to Him and me. I look up into His eyes and He winks and smiles at me. The name fits me perfectly and describes who I am in Christ. I've left my old name behind, along with the sin and trials it reminds me of. Christ has made me and then remade me. In eternity He will rename me.

**Take It to Heart**
Dear Lord, thank you for my new name. Thank you for new life in you. In Jesus's name, amen.

**Take It Further**
What names are used for Jesus in Scripture? List them below. How do each of these names describe how we relate to Him? Pray a prayer of thanksgiving through each name. For example, "Jesus, you are Savior. Thank you for saving me from sin."

# Be Intolerant: The Church of Thyatira

**Scripture Reading**: Revelation 2:18–29

**Key Verse**
"Nevertheless I have this against you: You tolerate that woman Jezebel, who calls herself a prophetess." Revelation 2:20

**Devotion**
At first I didn't see the scratch on my bumper because it was small and only on the surface. It would be no problem to put up with it. I just let it go. But time has gone by and the scratch is getting bigger. Rust is starting to creep in, too. I wish I would have taken care of it when it was small.

We tolerate a lot that we should take care of right away. You have a sore throat but no time to go to the doctor, so you just plow through your day. Two days later you can't muster the strength to get out of bed. You plan to pay the bills later, but you let them go past the due date. Now you have late fees to pay, too.

Jezebel declared herself a prophetess to the church of Thyatira. In reality she was influencing the church members to sin. The church leaders just put up with her even though the trouble she was causing started to snowball. Jesus instructed the church to get her out and repent from sin.

We need to do the same thing on a personal level. If we are dissatisfied with our spouse because of what we read or what we watch, we need to cut out those books or movies. If a friendship we are investing in is causing us to be discontent, critical, or gossipy, we need to spend less time with that friend.

Don't let sinful influences hang around. Repent, and get them out! Our world tells us to be tolerant, but when it comes to our spiritual lives, we are called to be intolerant.

**Take It to Heart**
Dear Lord, open my eyes to see what is urging me to sin. Give me the wisdom and self-control to cut out sinful influences from my life. In Jesus's name, amen.

**Take It Further**
John wrote to another church that needed to get the false teachers out. Read 2 John to learn more about how a church ought to be intolerant of false teachers. (It won't take long; 2 John is only one chapter long!) What two words are repeated often in 2 John? How do these two words relate to being intolerant of sinful influences and false teachers?

# Wake Up: The Church of Sardis

**Scripture Reading**: Revelation 3:1–6

**Key Verse**
"Wake up! Strengthen what remains and is about to die, for I have not found your deeds complete in the sight of my God." Revelation 3:2

**Devotion**
Ben Franklin devised a system to live a morally perfect life. He carried a small notebook with him; inside the notebook was a list of thirteen virtues: temperance, silence, order, resolution, industry, sincerity, justice, moderation, cleanliness, tranquility, chastity, and humility. Every day he evaluated his behavior in each category and made

a black mark in the column next to the virtue where he made an offense. Order was the hardest for him to keep. He had a hard time organizing his papers and finding places for his things to belong. He also had a hard time keeping a consistent schedule since he needed to be flexible and meet with people when they were available. Eventually he gave up trying to be orderly since he could not reach perfection despite his best efforts.[2]

Jesus gives each of the seven churches in Revelation a short list of what they need to do to improve. The church of Sardis is told to wake up and to strengthen what remains. I imagine the church of Sardis cutting back on sleep and exercising their hearts out like they are training for the Iron Man competition. Exhausted and overwhelmed, they never reach perfection despite all their hard work.

Many sections in Scripture contain lists of direct commands. The Ten Commandments. The Sermon on the Mount. Every Sunday sermon leaves us with a list of application points to put into practice. Then we get to work, focusing on each of these commands and striving for perfection.

But obedience to God cannot be fulfilled by our own strength, but by the Holy Spirit's work in

---

2 *The Autobiography of Benjamin Franklin*, 41, https://www.ushistory.org/franklin/autobiography/page41.htm, accessed 20 June 2020

us. This message to the church of Sardis is sandwiched between the seven spirits in Jesus's hand and a call to listen to what the Spirit is saying.

The Holy Spirit is the one with the power to change us. If we want to obey what God says, we need to yield to His work in our lives.

**Take It to Heart**
Our God in heaven, thank you for sending the Holy Spirit. May I rely on Him and not on my own strength for daily obedience to you. In Jesus's name, amen.

**Take It Further**
What do these verses say about the work of the Holy Spirit in a believer's life? What other verses describe the Holy Spirit? Start with John 14:6, Romans 8:26, Romans 15:13, and Galatians 5:22–23.

# Security Guard: The Church of Philadelphia

**Scripture Reading**: Revelation 3:7–13

**Key Verse**
"To the angel of the church in Philadelphia write: These are the words of him who is holy and true, who holds the key of David. What he opens no one can shut, and what he shuts no one can open." Revelation 3:7

**Devotion**
In 1908 the tallest building in the world was completed. The Singer Building in New York City was 612 feet tall, with forty-seven stories. Although the Singer Building only retained the title of the tallest building for one year, it does still hold the

record for the tallest building ever demolished. In 1968, the Singer Building was taken down to make way for the US Steel building known as 1 Liberty Plaza.

Before the building was demolished, security guards took a look through the building to be sure that everyone was out. They wanted to make sure no one would be accidentally crushed to death by the rubble of the building. Once the security guards swept the building, they stood watch to make sure no one entered it.

When Jesus describes Himself to the church of Philadelphia as the one holding the key of David, we remember Eliakim, King Hezekiah's palace security guard. In Isaiah 22:22, the Lord says Eliakim will have the key of the house of David. Jesus is asking us to picture Him as a security guard.

As we dive further into the book of Revelation, we will witness many scenes of judgment. As believers in Jesus Christ we do not need to feel fearful about the judgment described. The seals, trumpets, and bowls are designed to catch the attention of unbelievers, not to punish believers. Even before the Great White Throne (Rev. 20:11–15), we can stand with confidence because we trust in Christ, our perfect security guard. He will not make any mistakes about who is to go where for all eternity.

Instead of approaching the book of Revelation with trepidation, we can allow the portions of judgment to stir within us an urgency to share the good news of Jesus with our unbelieving family and friends. We can also be thankful to the Lord for His grace and mercy in rescuing us from the judgment to come.

**Take It to Heart**
Dear Lord, thank you for Jesus, the perfect security guard. Help me to rest in Him. Thank you for rescuing me from judgment both now and in the future. In Jesus's name, amen.

**Take It Further**
Do you have unbelieving family or friends? They will face this judgment unless they believe. Whom is God laying on your heart to share His message of salvation with?

# Staying Dependent on Jesus in Comfortable Times: The Church of Laodicea

**Scripture Reading**: Revelation 3:14–22

**Key Verse**

"I counsel you to buy from me gold refined in the fire, so you can become rich; and white clothes to wear, so you can cover your shameful nakedness; and salve to put on your eyes, so you can see." Revelation 3:18

**Devotion**

Laodicea was all set. They didn't need anything from anybody—which was exactly their problem, from God's perspective. Their financial independence had affected their attitude toward their walk with Jesus. They were lukewarm, just like the tepid water piped into the city for daily use.[3]

They were wealthy. When their city was destroyed by an earthquake, Rome offered to rebuild it but the Laodiceans said no, because they could afford to rebuild it themselves. They were wealthy because of their three main industries: Their banking center included a gold exchange. The special cloth they wove was famous in the Roman world. And their medical school was known for its special eye salve called Phyrigian powder, which was made from a stone found in Laodicea.

Jesus was calling the self-sufficient Laodiceans to come to Him for gold, clothing, and for eye salve. In other words, He wanted them to recognize their need for Him, the source of all their rich supplies.

When things are going well for us financially and it's easy to go out to the store and buy what we need, we forget that we are dependent on Christ for all we have. That self-reliant attitude carries over to our spiritual lives, too, when we think we are innately good people. But Jesus calls us to spend time with Him since He is the source

---

3  Ray Vander Laan, "Laodicea," *That the World May Know*, https://www.thattheworldmayknow.com/laodicea, accessed on 23 April 2020.

of our salvation and our sanctification. We grow in Christ by spending time with Him.

**Take It to Heart**

Thank you, Lord, for supplying my physical and spiritual needs. May I remember I am dependent on you even in comfortable times. In Jesus's name, amen.

**Take It Further**

Read Matthew 19:16–30. Why is it hard for a rich person to rely on Jesus for salvation? What obstacles do he or she face?

# The Throne

**Scripture Reading**: Revelation 4:1–11

**Key Verse**
"At once I was in the Spirit, and there before me was a throne in heaven with someone sitting on it." Revelation 4:2

**Devotion**
There have been many famous thrones in history. One is the Dragon Throne from the Forbidden City in China. The twelve gold dragons on its back look down on the throne while the body of the throne is decorated with designs of dragons and lotus petals. The United Kingdom has King Edward's Chair, with its high, pointed wooden back and golden lions for feet. It has been used as the coronation chair since 1296, Queen Elizabeth

II being the most recent monarch to be crowned while sitting on it.

Although there isn't a description of God's throne itself in Revelation 4, the throne is meant to be the center of attention. The word "throne" is mentioned twelve times in these eleven verses.

God on the throne is compared to brilliant jewels. There is a rainbow above it and thunder and lightning coming from it. There is a smooth sea, like crystal, in front of the throne. The creatures surround the throne and the elders bow down before it and lay their crowns before it. It is a majestic scene. I imagine it is even more stunning than John described since he was limited by language. The colors and the creatures and the opulence all climax into a remarkable scene of worship.

Although we do not physically see the beauty of the Lord on His throne yet, we see His beauty in nature, in His hand in our lives, and in our corporate worship in our local churches. Let the picture of God on His throne wash over you and move you to worship.

## Take It to Heart

Dear God in heaven, I stand in awe of your beauty and I ascribe to you glory, honor, power, and thanks. In Jesus' Name, Amen.

## Take It Further

Draw a picture of the throne room as described in Revelation 4. Use stick figures if you are not an artist! You can also look up other descriptions of God's throne room in Isaiah 6:1, Ezekiel 1:26, and Ezekiel 10:1.

# The Blood

**Scripture Reading**: Revelation 5:1–14

**Key Verse**

"And they sang a new song, saying: 'You are worthy to take the scroll and to open its seals, because you were slain, and with your blood you purchased men for God from every tribe and language and people and nation.'" Revelation 5:9

**Devotion**

Did you ever notice how often Christians sing about blood? *There Is Power in the Blood*. What can wash away my sin? *Nothing but the Blood. The Blood Will Never Lose Its Power*. We thank Jesus that *His Blood Ran Down* and covered us. *O, the Blood of Jesus!*

One Sunday while I was worshiping in church, there was a first-time visitor standing in front of me. We started to sing one of these songs about the blood of Jesus and I got uncomfortable. What was the visitor thinking? If Christianity is new to him, will he be turned off by all this blood talk? It's not common to sing and talk about blood in everyday life. I wondered if we should forget the "blood" songs and stick to songs about God's love, mercy, and forgiveness.

But passages like Revelation 5 changed my mind. Jesus's shed blood is crucial to the gospel. His blood is the currency used to purchase His people for God. There is no need to be embarrassed about the blood. We sing about His blood with joy and thanksgiving because without it we are lost.

In addition, Jesus's shed blood makes Him worthy to take the scroll from God's right hand and to open its seals. Not just anyone could open the scroll. Jesus is the only one who was worthy.

Jesus, who is God and man, lived a perfect life, died in our place, and rose again so everyone who believes in Him can have eternal life. Living a perfect life was not enough to make Him worthy: He needed to both live a perfect life and spill His blood in sacrifice. I don't need to shy away from the blood while sharing the gospel or worshiping.

I can unashamedly worship Jesus, the Lamb who was slain.

**Take It to Heart**
Oh Lord God, thank you for the blood of the Lamb. May I boldly proclaim the blood of Jesus which has given me forgiveness from all my sin. In Jesus' Name, Amen.

**Take It Further**
The descriptions of Jesus in Revelation 5:5 are familiar to us from other passages of Scripture. Write down here (or add to your list from Day 2) the descriptions from this verse. Then list similar verses from other parts of Scripture.

# God Is in Control

**Scripture Reading**: Revelation 6:1–17

**Key Verse**
"For the great day of their wrath has come, and who can stand?" Revelation 6:17

**Devotion**
Do you fear the book of Revelation because you picture God's judgment like the end of an action movie where everything is in mass chaos? Contrary to how it may seem, Revelation 6 does not give us a picture of mass chaos. God clearly has a plan:

- In verse 2, the rider of the white horse (who is probably the Antichrist) is given a crown. He did not steal it, and God is not surprised that the rider has it.

- In verse 4, the rider of the red horse is permitted or given power to take peace from the earth. They do not overpower God in their doings. This is part of God's plan.

- In verse 6, the price of grain is inflated one thousand percent, but God did not give the rider permission to destroy everything they wanted. The oil and the wine were left alone.

- In verse 10, the martyrs ask how long they have to wait until their death is avenged. They are told to wait because there is an appointed time. God has the judgment carefully planned out.

Although there is suffering, sadness, and death described in these six seals, this is not a free-for-all. God is in charge.

I trust God in His sovereignty over my daily life. God knows what will happen to me, and He has good plans. God in Revelation is the same God who can be trusted today.

Will believers today be eyewitnesses to the events of Revelation 6? I don't know. But if we are here to witness it, I know God's punishment is not for us. We are exempt from God's punishment because Jesus has already taken God's wrath in our place.

**Take It to Heart**
Thank you, Lord, that the end-times destruction is not for me. Thank you for rescuing me and teaching me not to fear. In Jesus's name, amen.

**Take It Further**
How do I know for sure God's wrath is not for believers in Him? Write out these verses below: John 3:36, Romans 2:5–6, and Romans 5:6–11.

# A Two-Way Street

**Scripture Reading**: Revelation 7:1–17

**Key Verse**
"For the Lamb in the center of the throne will be their shepherd; he will lead them to springs of living water. And God will wipe away every tear from their eyes." Revelation 7:17

**Devotion**
When you drive in a city you need to watch out for one-way street signs. All the traffic points in the same direction on a one-way street. There is no chance of meeting another vehicle face-to-face.

When we saw heaven's throne room in Revelation 4, we saw the elders and the creatures continually singing praises to God while He sat motionless on His throne. Most of the time, this is our picture of heaven: a stoic God giving no reaction to the praise He is receiving. This makes heaven sound boring and impersonal. It's like a one-way-street relationship, in which we are doing all the work while He just sits there.

In Revelation 7 we see a more detailed picture of the throne room of heaven. First there are the 144,000 people from the tribes of Israel. Then there is a multitude of people from every tribe, tongue, and nation. There are angels who join the elders and the four living creatures in worship. This great crowd in heaven is bringing praise to God and to the Lamb.

But this time God does not remain passive. He spreads out His protection over His people. He wipes away their tears while the Lamb guides them to springs of living water.

God's relationship with us is a two-way street, even in eternity. This is easy to forget while we are here on earth praising and serving yet not able to physically see God's movements toward us. But if you have trusted Christ as your Savior, God is on His throne, face-to-face with you, delighting in your praise, and leaning forward to give you protection, provision, and peace.

**Take It to Heart**
Our Father who is in heaven, hallowed be your name. Thank you for your protection, provision, and peace both now and in all eternity. In the name of the Lamb, amen.

**Take It Further**
What difference does it make to your expectations of heaven to picture God as active and not passive?

# The Prayers of the Saints

**Scripture Reading**: Revelation 8:1–5

**Key Verse**
"The smoke of the incense, together with the prayers of the saints, went up before God from the angel's hand." Revelation 8:4

**Devotion**
One of my favorite parts of a fireworks display are the fireworks that start out with one large burst before falling to the earth in streams of light. Just when you think the light will peter out, one of the stray sizzles bursts into a new ball of light. This kind of firework reminds me of the seals, trumpets, and bowls of Revelation. Revelation

6 showed us the first six seals. Chapter 8 shows us the seventh seal, which bursts into the seven trumpets. Later we will see the seventh trumpet burst into the seven bowls.

When the seventh seal is opened, there is silence for a half an hour. Then the prayers of the saints and incense waft up before God from the censer in the angel's hand. Immediately after the prayers, the angel scoops up the fire and throws it toward earth. This creates thunder, lightning, and an earthquake.

God hears our prayers. It may not always feel like it, but when we pray, our prayers waft up and appear before Him on His throne. Although we don't understand how it works, God moves in response to our prayers. God has chosen to make the prayers of His people part of His sovereign plan. It doesn't always feel that way. How can our prayers make any difference if God has everything planned out? I don't know, but God has asked us to pray. He has instructed us to pray. And He responds with an answer to our prayers. 1 John 5:14 says, "This is the confidence we have in approaching God: that if we ask anything according to his will, he hears us." Our prayers matter.

**Take It to Heart**

Dear God in heaven, thank you for inviting us to pray to you. I don't understand how prayer works, but I will be faithful and pray to you just as you asked. In Jesus's name, amen.

**Take It Further**

What has God laid on your heart to pray about lately? An unsaved family member or friend? An impossible situation? Instead of fretting, pray. Below, write a prayer or a list of what you want to pray about each day this week. Imagine your prayers floating up to heaven directly to God on His throne.

# Discipline for Repentance

**Scripture Reading**: Revelation 8:6–9:21

**Key Verse**
"The rest of mankind who were not killed by these plagues still did not repent of the work of their hands." Revelation 9:20

**Devotion**
I remember the first time I had to discipline my son. He was toddling around our living room like usual. Then he stopped and noticed something new: the electrical outlet. He squatted down and started to pick at the outlet covers. I cleared my throat and for the first time said the word I would repeat often as a parent.

No.

When a parent says "no," the child doesn't always stop. Sometimes it's necessary to take a bigger step to get the kid's attention so you can train them to do what is safe or right. For my kids, a firm, calm thump on the hand worked when they were toddlers. Now my kids are older and they respond to time alone in their room or taking away their screen time. The goal of my discipline is not to see my child suffer; I want them to turn away from harmful choices and choose obedience.

In a similar way, the seal, trumpet, and bowl judgments are designed by the Lord to get people's attention. The trumpet judgments are more severe than the seal judgments from chapter 6, yet they are still in God's plan and control. They are not an unleashing of unbridled fury.

God is not like a kid burning an ant with a magnifying glass, taking pleasure in the destruction from the trumpet judgments. God gives more severe destruction because He is trying to get the attention of unbelievers. God loves His creation and longs to see people come to Him in repentance. This is why God is "taking so long" to send Jesus back to earth. 2 Peter 3:9 says, "He is patient with you, not wanting anyone to perish, but everyone to come to repentance."

**Take It to Heart**

Dear God, thank you for your patience. I pray for my friend or family member _____, who needs to repent and come to you for salvation. I pray they would hear the gospel clearly and plainly. Empower me to take every opportunity to share Jesus with them. In Jesus's name, amen.

**Take It Further**

The "Romans Road" is a short list of verses that can help you explain the gospel simply and clearly. Write out the following verses: Romans 3:23, Romans 5:8, Romans 6:23, and Romans 10:9. You can also write a short explanation of how you would use these verses to explain salvation to your unbelieving family member or friend.

# What You Do Not Need to Know

**Scripture Reading**: Revelation 10:1–11

**Key Verse**
"And when the seven thunders spoke, I was about to write, but I heard a voice from heaven say, 'Seal up what the seven thunders have said and do not write it down.'" Revelation 10:4

**Devotion**
I keep two calendars. The calendar in my phone is for all my appointments and for all the kids' activities, too. My phone calendar syncs with my husband's phone calendar so we don't double-book ourselves. My second calendar is a paper calendar on the pantry door. This is the kids' calendar,

where I make note of band lessons, days off school, and Saturday family plans so they know what to expect.

I do not put every entry from my phone calendar onto the kids' calendar. I don't want to overwhelm them with too much. I just want them to know what they need to know.

For some reason, John needed to hear the seven thunders, but we do not. I do not know why, but just as my kids trust me to tell them exactly what they need to know, I trust God to tell us what we need to know. God, in His mercy, does not overwhelm us with too much.

And what should we do with what God does tell us? We need to digest it and share it. John was asked to eat the scroll. It was sweet at first but turned sour in his stomach. So much of God's word is sweet, but there are bitter parts, too, like the heartbreaking disobedience of Israel in Judges and Kings and Samuel. Like the truth that we are all sinners in need of a Savior. But these bitter sections of Scripture compel us to share the truth so that our friends and family can turn to Jesus and escape God's judgment.

**Take It to Heart**

Thank you, God, for giving us everything we need to know for life and godliness (2 Peter 1:3). May I be diligent to digest your word and faithful to share your truth. In Jesus's name, amen.

**Take It Further**

What other Scriptures describe taking in God's word as eating? Start with Psalm 34:8 and 1 Peter 2:2.

# The Witnesses

**Scripture Reading**: Revelation 11:1–14

**Key Verse**
"And I will give power to my two witnesses..."
Revelation 11:3

**Devotion**
Is this passage to be taken literally or figuratively? First there is a temple. Is it one of the literal temples like Zerubbabel's, or is it talking about the church in figurative language?

Then there are the two witnesses. They sound a lot like some Old Testament prophets. Like Elijah, they will have power to shut up the sky so there is no rain. Like Moses, they will have power to turn water into blood. John tells us he is using figurative language when he refers to Jerusalem as

Egypt and Sodom. Does that mean the rest of the numbers and symbols and images in this passage are figurative, too? We don't know for sure.

One thing is for sure: the witnesses are called to testify. Then they experience suffering and even death. But death is not the end. God gives them the breath of life. They are resurrected and go up to heaven to live eternally.

God has given each one of His believers the command to witness. God promised that we will experience suffering here on earth (John 16:33). We will also die (unless the Lord returns first!). But our bodily death is not the end. We will be given new life in heaven with God forever.

Just as God empowered His two witnesses in Revelation 11, God has given us power through the Holy Spirit as we witness for Him. Jesus promised His apostles, "You will receive power when the Holy Spirit comes on you; and you will be my witnesses in Jerusalem, and in all Judea and Samaria, and to the ends of the earth" (Acts 1:8).

**Take It to Heart**

Our Father in heaven, thank you for the Holy Spirit who gives power to witness in your name. May I rely on His strength as I share the good news of Jesus with my family and friends. In Jesus's name, amen.

**Take It Further**

The Bible is to be taken literally, yet it uses figurative language. Remind yourself of these figurative language constructs. Write down a definition and find a biblical example of each of the following types of figurative language: simile, metaphor, personification, hyperbole, proverb, parable.

# Small but Not Insignificant

**Scripture Reading:** Revelation 11:15–19

**Key Verse**
"The time has come for judging the dead and for rewarding your servants the prophets and your saints and those who reverence your name both small and great..." Revelation 11:18

**Devotion**
In 1665, English scientist Robert Hooke published *Micrographia,* which contains detailed drawings of hundreds of things he observed under his microscope including the first drawings of cells. Most of the world had never seen the tiny goings-on of plants and other specimens until reading Hooke's

book. Now the existence of cells is common knowledge. The microscopic world is arranged to create the world as we know it—everything our eyes see.

When God in heaven says He rewards both the small and the great, the Greek word for small is *micros*. This is the same Greek root word from which we get the English words "microscope" and "microcosm." We have an idea of just how small we are talking when we hear the word "micro."

Most of the time, I feel like my life is micro. I serve in my small church. I love my family and friends and even my neighbors. But what difference can all of this make? The world is so big and there are so many people out there who are doing big things for God. Does anyone notice the small things I do?

Yes. God notices all the little things I do that show I revere His name. He notices when I teach Sunday School even when there are only a handful of kids who come. He notices when I turn the channel so I don't hear His name raked through the mud.

Even if I feel like no one else notices, God does. He doesn't even need a microscope to detect it. And He opens heaven for those who revere Him, to dwell with Him in the heavenly temple forever.

**Take It to Heart**

"Dear God in heaven, thank you for noticing and rewarding the small and the great. May I revere your name with my lips and in my heart. In Jesus's name, amen.

**Take It Further**

Where in the Bible does God notice small things? List them here and draw a picture illustrating how they revered God's name. Who in your life does small things for God?

# The End of Timid Testimonies

**Scripture Reading**: Revelation 12:1–13:1

**Key Verse**
"They overcame him by the blood of the Lamb and by the word of their testimony..." Revelation 12:11

**Devotion**
I'm just an ordinary Christian with an unremarkable testimony. I was born into a Christian home. Went to church and heard about Jesus. Got saved as a child. End of testimony. I never rebelled and nothing crazy ever happened to me. Dramatic salvation stories always wow me, but they also make

me feel boring. But John says there is more to my testimony than my ho-hum experience.

After the seventh trumpet in chapter 11 and before the bowl judgments in chapter 16, John describes several signs in heaven. Just like a street sign points to something else, so do the key players in this sign.

- **The woman represents Israel**. The sun, moon, and stars remind us of Joseph's dream. There are twelve stars, one for each tribe of Israel.

- **The child is Jesus**. Jesus is racially Jewish. Revelation 12:5 says He will rule all the nations with an iron scepter, just how Psalm 2:9 describes the Messiah. The child is snatched up to God; in other words, He ascends into the heavens.

- **The dragon is Satan**. We don't need any detective work here; John tells us in verse 9. Although Satan fights, he is not strong enough. He is called the serpent and the devil who leads the whole world astray. He is also called the accuser.

How can I overcome the accuser? What if my testimony isn't powerful enough?

If I feel my testimony isn't powerful enough, I am putting more emphasis on my experience than on the blood of the Lamb. I don't need to have a drama-filled testimony in order for it to be powerful. The blood of the Lamb is the power of any testimony.

**Take It to Heart**
Dear God in heaven, thank you that the accuser has no power over me. I testify that the blood of the Lamb has saved me and given me boldness to stand before God on His throne. In Jesus's name, amen.

**Take It Further**
How did you come to trust in Jesus Christ as your Savior? Write your testimony below. When you have written it, share it on social media or with a friend.

# The Source of the Sign

**Scripture Reading**: Revelation 13:2–13:18

**Key Verse**
"This calls for wisdom..." Revelation 13:18

**Devotion**
One day I was chatting with a group of moms at a birthday party. In the conversation, I mentioned that I am a Christian and my husband is a pastor. Then one of the moms said, "Let me ask you something. One time I was at a séance and the woman told me my grandmother would send me a sign. She would send me a butterfly. I was shocked because my grandmother loved butterflies, but the medium had no way of knowing. As soon as the session was over and I walked out to my car, a butterfly fluttered by my head even though there

weren't any flowers around and it wasn't the right season for them. I was freaked out. Tell me: was this real?"

I stammered something and tried to bring the conversation back to God, but I'm not sure I knew how to answer her until I read this portion of Revelation.

The beast of the earth is part of the unholy trinity that consists of Satan, the beast of the sea, and the beast of the earth. The beast of the earth performs signs like healings, and even fire coming down from heaven. These signs are factually reported, so they are real. But who are these signs from? They are not from God.

When you hear about miracles or unexplainable things, the right question to ask is not "Is this real?" but "Whom is this from?" The source of the sign determines the nature of the sign and its purpose. If the sign or miracle points you to Jesus, then it is from God. But if it points you away from God and distracts the witness from Jesus, then the sign is not from God.

**Take It to Heart**

Dear Lord God, I hear reports of unexplainable things and I don't always know what to make of them. Give me wisdom and discernment to know when a sign or wonder is from you. In Jesus's name, amen.

**Take It Further**

Read Deuteronomy 13:1–5. How did God tell His people to discern whether or not a miraculous sign was really from Him?

# A Faith That Will Not Fail

**Scripture Reading:** Revelation 14:1-20

**Key Verse**
"This calls for patient endurance on the part of the saints who obey God's commandments and remain faithful to Jesus." Revelation 14:12

**Devotion**
Between November 2018 and October 2019, Nigeria was the country with the most martyrdoms in the world, with 1,350 confirmed Christian martyrs and 224 confirmed abductions of Christians. And these are only the *confirmed* instances of persecution. Pastors and Christian leaders in the nation are protesting and pleading

with their government to protect their lives.[4] One pastor asked the Western world for help so they would not be wiped out. The persecution has been labeled a genocide. The pastor also asked us to pray that their faith would not fail.[5]

After a glimpse of the 144,000 believers in heaven, three angels come to earth with three messages. The first angel shares the gospel and invites people to turn to God. The second angel announces the fall of Babylon. Babylon was one of the enemies of Israel, but in John's day of persecution, Christians used the term Babylon as a nickname for Rome. Here we can understand it as referring to all evil in the world. The third angel announces that the full strength of God's wrath is coming.

Although we do not know whether we will be part of the believers who are here on earth at this time, John says believers are called to patiently endure while obeying God's commandments and

---

4 Jayson Casper, "All Across Nigeria, Christians Marched Sunday to Protest Persecution," *Christianity Today*, Feb. 3, 2020, https://www.christianitytoday.com/news/2020/february/nigeria-christian-prayer-walk-can-enoch-adeboye-buhari.html, accessed on June 20, 2020.

5 J. Lee Grady, "Nigeria's Persecuted Christians Are Begging Us for Help," *Charisma News*, Jan. 15, 2020, https://www.charismanews.com/opinion/79522-nigeria-s-persecuted-christians-are-begging-us-for-help, accessed on May 12, 2020.

remaining faithful to Jesus. God notices the believers in persecution and going through hard times who are weary and worn out. He calls us to keep on and not to give up.

If you are facing a hard time, continue on in the Lord. Rely on the Lord for strength so you can patiently endure until, at just the right time, He brings you home to heaven and He gives justice to evil.

### Take It to Heart

Dear Lord, I pray for the persecuted Christians in Nigeria and around the world to have patient endurance. I pray that I would continue on in obedience to the Lord and in faith when I feel like giving up. In Jesus's name, amen.

### Take It Further

You can send encouraging notes to the persecuted Christians in Nigeria and let them know they are not forgotten by their brothers and sisters in Christ from around the world. Go to Persecution.com, the website of Voice of the Martyrs, and see how you can pray specifically for them and how you can write to them.

# Worship God in Response to His Wrath

**Scripture Reading**: Revelation 15:1–8

**Key Verse**
"Great and marvelous are your deeds, Lord God Almighty. Just and true are your ways, King of the ages." Revelation 15:3

**Devotion**
In corporate worship we are motivated to sing praises to God because of who He is and what He has done. We sing about His love, forgiveness, and mercy. We sing about how He created the world and has given us salvation. But how often do we sing praises to God because of His wrath?

Most of the time, we are embarrassed about God's wrath. We try to hide God and His wrath like we would a crazy old uncle with a temper issue: we love him, but we hope the word doesn't get out that we are actually related.

Yet, in the heavens, the seven angels bring out the bowls of God's wrath (also called the plagues), and those who are victorious sing praises to God in response to His wrath. God's wrath shows that God is just and true. He is in charge. Many of us have seen parents who never follow through on threatened discipline with their kids. What is the result? Those kids know they can get away with anything. In a similar way, a God without justice and wrath is not the King.

We do not need to be ashamed of God's wrath. For believers, Jesus's death on the cross soothed God's wrath (1 John 2:2). For unbelievers, God is patient, waiting until the last days to pour out the last of His wrath. He is waiting for unbelievers to come to Him in repentance. But for those who do not come, God's wrath will give out justice. God's wrath shows Him as King. As believers, we worship the King and give glory to His name.

**Take It to Heart**

Dear God in heaven, I worship you because you are just and true. You are the King, and it is right for you to give your wrath. Thank you for providing a way of escape for me. I pray that my family and friends will experience your salvation and this way of escape as well. In Jesus's name, amen.

**Take It Further**

Can you think of any hymns or worship songs that talk about God's wrath? If so, write them below. You can search online or on YouTube to find lyrics to songs. Start with *O Worship the King*.

# Full Wrath Measured Out

**Scripture Reading**: Revelation 16:1–21

**Key Verse**
"The seventh angel poured out his bowl into the air, and out of the temple came a loud voice from the throne, saying, 'It is done!'" Revelation 16:17

**Devotion**
I don't buy orange juice very often, but when I do, it's usually for a recipe. Without fail, the kids open the fridge looking for something to snack on and yell, "Mom! Can I have some orange juice?"

I reply, "No. I'm reserving it for a recipe. Once I'm done with the recipe, then I will pour out the rest for you."

Finally the day comes when I'm making smoothies or marinating chicken and I use the portion of the juice I was holding back. Then I pour out the rest into four glasses, one for each kid, and let them drink.

When I first read that the bowl judgments are brimming with God's wrath, I had a picture of unbridled fury—like when my kids are being loud and draining my energy and I'm trying to stay calm until I just can't take it anymore, and I yell at the top of my lungs.

God's wrath is anger, but it's not the same as my outbursts on my bad days. Wrath is divine punishment based on God's judgment against someone. Wrath is intense rage, yet, in God's case, it is not out of control. Although God is filled with an emotion of anger toward those who worship the beast, that anger is justified. When God's wrath is being poured out from the bowls, it is not unbridled fury. It has been measured out. Part of it was poured out through the seals and the trumpet judgments. Now He is pouring out the rest, which had previously been held back. The time has come to use it up.

God's wrath is premeasured and preplanned. He has held it back as long as He can, but in Revelation 16, the time has come to pour out the rest so that His kingdom can come.

**Take It to Heart**

"Dear God, thank you for sending Jesus to soothe your wrath toward me. Thank you for setting things right at the end of time in your justice and your righteous anger. In Jesus's name, amen."

**Take It Further**

What other places in Scripture describe God's wrath as a cup brimming over?

# Babylon

**Scripture Reading**: Revelation 17:1–18

**Key Verse**

"For God has put it into their hearts to accomplish his purpose by agreeing to give the beast their power to rule, until God's words are fulfilled." Revelation 17:17

**Devotion**

When Babylon is mentioned in the New Testament in Revelation and in 1 Peter 5:13, it is most likely a code word for Rome, the government that was persecuting Christians in John and Peter's day. Why didn't they just come out and say Rome if they meant Rome? Because when the New Testament letters were passed around, the Christians would be in even more danger if they were found to have said disparaging things about the government, so they used the word "Babylon" to refer to the idolatrous world power of their day. However, this scene in Revelation 17 is yet future. Here, John uses the name Babylon to describe the evil world power of whenever this scene takes place.

In the Old Testament, Babylon was the world power that conquered the nation of Judah in 586 BC. But Babylon did not stay on top. The Persian empire conquered Babylon, and then one of the Persian kings sent back a group of Israelites to rebuild the ruined temple and the broken walls around Jerusalem. For a period of history, it looked like evil had won. It looked like Babylon had overpowered God's people forever, but it was all in God's plan. He redeemed and restored His people at just the right time.

There will always be a Babylon. There will always be evil powers who look like they are winning against God's goodness. When the Israelites were exiled from their land, God was in control. When Rome rose to power in the first century, God was in control. The dark times fit into His plan.

## Take It to Heart

Dear Lord, thank you for being sovereign. I know you will overcome evil with good. Keep me from despair. Keep me away from participating in the evil around me. In Jesus's name, amen.

## Take It Further

Read the book of Habakkuk. It won't take long since it only has three chapters. God tells Habakkuk that He is sending the nation of Babylon to conquer Judah. How is Babylon described in chapter 2? What will happen to Babylon after they have conquered Judah?

# Sinking Like a Millstone

**Scripture Reading**: Revelation 18:1–24

**Key Verse**
"Woe! Woe, O great city, where all who had ships on the sea became rich through her wealth! In one hour she has been brought to ruin!" Revelation 18:19

**Devotion**
Our family likes to walk on the winding path along the creek in the woods. Sometimes we stop and play at the creek's edge and I try to skip rocks. I'm not very good at it. I fling the stone, and—*plop*—it's gone so quickly! No one really notices because the stone was so small and so was its splash. But if I were to hurl a 1,500-pound millstone into the creek, everyone would notice! The

big splash would rival any cannonball contest off the high dive at the neighborhood pool. And the stone would sink so far down it would never be found again.

Babylon, personified as a wicked woman, is wrapped up in selfishness. She lives to draw attention to herself and to indulge her sensuous pleasures (18:7). She lives in excessive luxury (18:11–16) while there are poor people struggling to get enough to eat. And what will come of her luxurious living? Nothing. It'll be gone in an hour, just like a millstone will quickly sink to the bottom of the sea.

Selfish living is not compatible with Christian living. Saving for the future with wise spending and investing is wisdom, but hoarding like Ebenezer Scrooge is selfish. Spending time to rest is wisdom, but always looking forward to the next break so you can indulge your desires is selfish. Spending money on over-the-top luxuries while ignoring the poor is selfish.

Jesus Christ showed us the ultimate act of unselfishness when He left heaven to die for our sake. In response to Him, we can live generously, unselfishly spending time on what will last.

**Take It to Heart**
Dear Lord God, thank you for the unselfish sacrifice of your death on the cross. Give me wisdom on how to live selflessly. In Jesus's name, amen.

**Take It Further**
Babylon is destroyed in part because they did not live justly. They oppressed the poor around them. What does God have to say about living justly? Find three Bible verses that mention justice.

# Prepping for the Battle

**Scripture Reading**: Revelation 19:1–21

**Key Verse**
"After this I heard what sounded like the roar of a great multitude in heaven shouting: 'Hallelujah! Salvation and glory and power belong to our God...'" Revelation 19:1

**Devotion**
We have finally come to the end of life on earth as we know it. This is the part people refer to when they say, "I read the end. Jesus wins." Although movie makers film the Armageddon scene as a long, drawn out battle, it's over pretty quickly. Jesus comes riding on His white horse, and the armies of heaven fight alongside him. The armies of heaven could possibly be angels, or they could

be the righteous, His believers dressed in white who are mentioned earlier in the chapter.

If they are indeed believers, what stands out to me is the way Jesus prepares them to fight with Him at this last battle:

- **Corporate worship**. The multitude in heaven worships God in heaven with a full Hallelujah unparalleled in Scripture. Revelation 19:1–8 is the only place where this Greek word is used.

- **Feasting**. It's always good to carb up before a big physical event. God gives the marriage supper of the Lamb before the big battle (Rev. 19:9).

- **Jesus's presence**. Jesus is physically present with us while we fight together at this last battle. He is leading the way while we follow Him. We can trust Him to lead the way into battle (Rev. 19:11–14).

The same preparations work for our spiritual battles today. When we worship in our local church, we remember we are not alone. We are the body of Christ. Come to church regularly and focus on worshiping the Lord and giving honor to His name. We can feast on God's Word and on Christ who is the Word of God. Jesus's presence is "with us always, even to the end of the age" (Matt. 28:20).

## Take It to Heart

Dear Lord, prepare my heart for spiritual battles through corporate worship, feasting on your Word, and your guiding presence. In the name of the Lamb, amen.

## Take It Further

Revelation 19 has a lot more description of Jesus. Add these to your descriptions of Jesus on the devotional from Day 2 or list it below. You can even draw a picture of Faithful and True on His white horse.

# Grace Removes the Shame of Sin

**Scripture Reading**: Revelation 20:1–15

**Key Verse**
"And I saw the dead, great and small, standing before the throne, and books were opened. Another book was opened, which is the book of life. The dead were judged according to what they had done as recorded in the books." Revelation 20:12

**Devotion**
When I was a teenager, I attended a retreat with an emotionally charged speaker. He was trying to motivate the audience to turn to Jesus for forgiveness and salvation by describing the final judgment. He asked us to picture standing before God

as He pulls out a large file full of cards. The sins I have done are listed on each card. The thought of my sins being publicly exposed was terrifying! Then the speaker said if we ask Jesus to forgive us, He marks each card with His blood as He forgives us, but my insecure, teenaged self was sure everyone could still read through the red stain to see the record of my sins.

Thankfully, this is not how the Bible describes the judgment. God opens not a card file, but two books. One is the book of the deeds of the dead. Only the sins of the spiritually dead, the unbelievers, are listed here. The other is the Book of Life. If you are a believer in Jesus Christ, like I was as a teen, then your name is in the Book of Life. You have no reason to fear that your sinful deeds will be exposed.

Our salvation doesn't just save us from hell. It saves us from the embarrassment and shame of sin.

We can offer this same grace to our brothers and sisters in Christ. If someone has wronged you but you have forgiven them, you should not gossip about it. Have the same grace with your children. Do not bring up their past sins once they have been forgiven. Do not post about them on social media for all to see. This is wisdom: "Whoever would foster love covers over an offense, but whoever repeats the matter separates close friends" (Prov. 17:9).

**Take It to Heart**
Dear Lord God, the Great Judge, thank you for your forgiveness and for covering over my sin. Thank you for writing my name in the Lamb's book of life. In Jesus's name, amen.

**Take It Further**
How else does the Bible describe the extent of God's forgiveness of our sins? Copy down Psalm 103:11–12 and Isaiah 43:25 to find out.

---

# What Makes Me Feel at Home

**Scripture Reading**: Revelation 21:1–27

**Key Verse**
"And I heard a loud voice from the throne saying, 'Look! God's dwelling place is now among the people, and he will dwell with them. They will be his people, and God himself will be with them and be their God.'" Revelation 21:3

**Devotion**
The new heaven and the new earth are going to be incredible beyond our wildest imaginations. There will be streets of gold, pearly gates, lush gardens, and a city roomy enough for all believers in Jesus Christ from all times in history. There

will be no darkness, sun, or moon since the glory of God gives it light.

Although new can be exciting, it also can feel unfamiliar.

Since we moved recently, the feeling of unfamiliar is still fresh in my mind. Our house is a wonderful old house with just the right sized yard and plenty of room for all our things. But I have no idea where anything is! The kids will ask me where something is, and it takes a long thought process and some hunting before I can answer them.

During our last move, I remember getting up the first morning to make breakfast. I bravely stepped into the kitchen, determined to get used to a new home. My husband found me ten minutes later, stuck, staring, frozen like a deer in headlights because I was completely overwhelmed with the unfamiliarity of my surroundings. I felt out of place all day long until my husband came home. I could feel my whole body relax the moment I heard his voice as he came in the door. Knowing he was there too made me feel like I belonged.

I imagine the new heaven and new earth will be the same way.

Although our surroundings will be unfamiliar, the very presence of Jesus Christ will be familiar to us. We know Him. He knows us. We are the bride of Christ and we belong.

## Take It to Heart

Dear Lord, thank you for being ever present. I am looking forward to being with you and seeing you face to face in the new heaven and the new earth. In Jesus's name, amen.

## Take It Further

What role does God's presence play in our life in this world? Refer to Exodus 33:14, Psalm 16:11, Psalm 23:4, Matthew 28:20, and any other verses you can find.

# A Garden and a City

**Scripture Reading**: Revelation 22:1–5

**Key Verse**
"Then the angel showed me the river of the water of life, as clear as crystal, flowing from the throne of God and of the Lamb down the middle of the great street of the city." Revelation 22:1–2a

**Devotion**
Our family has taken day trips into New York City. I love the history and culture there, but I miss the peace and quiet of the country. I feel lost on the crowded streets. The traffic is impatient. On the other hand, the rural areas I've visited have plenty of peace and quiet, but I miss the close proximity to shopping and events.

Most of the time, I hear the new heaven and new earth described as a return to the garden of Eden. Adam and Eve enjoyed peaceful face-to-face time with God while they tended their plants. They rested in the shade of the Tree of Life, which also appears in the new heaven and new earth. Both places boast a significant river and provide a sinless existence.

But the new heaven and new earth is described as a city as well as a garden.

Why a city and not just a garden? God's intention for the garden of Eden was for it to be full of people. God told Adam and Eve to be fruitful and multiply. Unfortunately, they sinned and were kicked out of the garden before they fulfilled that command.

Each generation of God's people is fulfilling the command to be fruitful and multiply not just by giving birth, but by sharing the gospel so others become born again. The new Jerusalem will be filled with a multitude of believers from every tribe, tongue, and nation. The fullness of God's people will worship Him together in community for all eternity.

The new heaven and new earth have the best of both worlds: the peace of God with the streets of gold.

**Take It to Heart**
Dear Lord, thank you for the beauty of the city of the new Jerusalem. I am looking forward to worshiping you in community with all of my brothers and sisters in Christ. In Jesus's name, amen.

**Take It Further**
If you live in a city, chose a rural area closest to you. If you live in a rural area, chose a city near you. Look online to find a church in the area and pray especially for its ministry there.

# Soon and Very Soon

**Scripture Reading:** Revelation 22:6–21

**Key Verse**
"Behold, I am coming soon! Blessed is he who keeps the words of the prophecy in this book."
Revelation 22:7

**Devotion**
What is the definition of the word "soon"? I asked around and here are the responses I received:

- About the same as right away

- Next few minutes

- Next few days

- Next week

- Next month

I also received a pessimistic answer: "If the person is undependable, maybe never."

Three times in Revelation 22, Jesus says He is coming soon. Two thousand years later, we may wonder what "soon" means to Jesus.

The Greek word used for "soon" in this passage can mean "without delay."

Jesus outlines the plan for the end of days. Although Christians disagree about which end-times timeline the Bible presents, we agree that His plan is working right on time.

Jesus is completely trustworthy. If He said He is coming soon, then He is coming soon. His definition of "soon" is different than what we expect in our human experience, but He is coming back right on time. Keep waiting. Keep watching. Keep taking His word to heart.

## Take It to Heart

Dear God, I look forward to you coming, right on time. Help me to obey you and worship you while I wait. In Jesus's name, amen.

## Take It Further

After you add to your list of the descriptions of Jesus, take a look back at your notes throughout this devotional journey. What lesson impacted you the most? What is your biggest takeaway from this time in the book of Revelation?

# Small Group Discussion Guide

Y ou can use this book together with a small group or Bible study group. This small group discussion guide can be used for a six-week period while discussing five days' worth of *Take It to Heart* devotions per week. Start with the Take It Further questions for each day. If you have more time, you can add the discussion questions below.

You can also use the short teaching videos available at ReadtheHardParts.com/Revelation (one per week).

### Week One (Days 1–5)

1. Who wrote Revelation? How did he get the information that is written in it? What is the purpose of the book of Revelation?

2. How would you feel if you were John and you saw Jesus as Light on the island of Patmos? What difference does it make in your life today to call Jesus the Light?

3. Why do you think the message to each church ends with "He who has an ear, let him hear what the Spirit says to the churches"?

## Week Two (Days 6–10)

1. Imagine Jesus is evaluating your church. What would he point out as strengths and weaknesses? Pray together about what you notice.

2. What stands out to you in the throne room of God? Why does that stand out and how does it impact your faith?

## Week Three (Days 11–15)

1. Who might the 144,000 be?

2. Destruction is hard to read about. We are thankful that although we all deserve destruction, God has rescued those who believe in Jesus Christ as Savior. What promises from Scripture remind you of God's mercy and salvation for you?

## Week Four (Days 16–20)

1. We don't know everything there is to know about heaven and the future. We only know what God has revealed to us. If you could ask God anything about heaven and the future, what would you want to know?

2. What was the purpose of the temple? How did having the temple influence and affect God's people?

## Week Five (Days 21–25)

1. In chapter 15, there are a lot of phrases that remind me of things that happened during Moses's time. Can you find any of them?
2. What words and phrases in these chapters show that this is the end, or the last of God's wrath?
3. How does worship help you focus on God during hard times?

## Week Six (Days 26–30)

1. When my husband and I were looking to buy a house, we toured a lot of homes. Then we would discuss what we noticed about the property. What do you notice from this tour of the new heavens and the new earth?
2. We are created with deep longings. We long for beauty, relationship with others, happiness, safety, love, and belonging. How will the new heavens and earth meet these longings?

# Acknowledgements

T hank you to all my Read the Hard Parts readers for being curious about the hard parts of Scripture. Thanks especially to the ladies' Sunday School classes at Whitehall Bible Fellowship Church and Bethany Bible Fellowship Church in Hatfield for studying Revelation with me. I am grateful to Bible Study Fellowship for their study of Revelation. Thank you for challenging your students to understand God's word and to take it to heart. Thank you to Rebecca Armstrong for your meticulous editing abilities and to Holly Splawn for encouraging me along the way.

# For Further Study

Arthur, Kay, and David Arthur, *Behold, Jesus Is Coming!*, Harvest House, 1995.

Arthur, Kay, and John C. Whitcomb, *The New Inductive Study Bible: Updated New American Standard Bible*, Harvest House, 2000.

Bible Study Fellowship International, bsfinternational.org

Keener, Craig S., *Revelation (NIV Application Commentary)*, Zondervan, 2000.

# About the Author

Rachel Schmoyer encourages Christians to find simple truth in complex parts of Scripture through her writing and speaking ministry *Read the Hard Parts*. She is a pastor's wife and mom of four from the Lehigh Valley of Pennsylvania. She holds a BS in Bible and a BS in Education from Cairn University. You can connect with Rachel online at ReadtheHardParts.com or on Facebook, Instagram, Twitter, or Pinterest.

WWW.READTHEHARDPARTS.COM

**Free Printable Bible Reading Record Chart available at ReadtheHardParts.com**

A no-stress, no-pressure way to read the whole Bible. Simply mark off each chapter as you read at your own pace.

Printed in the United States
By Bookmasters